August Kleinzahler's first three collections are *Green Sees Things in Waves* and *Red Sauce, Whiskey and Snow*. He lives in San Francisco, where he writes a music column for the *San Diego Weekly Reader*.

AUGUST KLEINZAHLER

Live from
the Hong Kong Nile Club

Poems 1975–1990

faber and faber

First published in the USA in 2000
by Farrar, Straus and Giroux
First published in Great Britain in 2000
by Faber and Faber Limited
3 Queen Square London WC1N 3AU

Typeset by Faber and Faber Ltd
Printed in England by MPG Books Ltd, Bodmin, Cornwall

© August Kleinzahler, 2000

August Kleinzahler is hereby identified as author of this
work in accordance with Section 77 of the Copyright,
Designs and Patents Act 1988

A CIP record for this book
is available from the British Library

ISBN 0-571-20428-7

10 9 8 7 6 5 4 3 2 1

In memory of my brother, Harris

Acknowledgments

Some of these poems first appeared in the following magazines:

Brief, Cimarron Review, Epoch, Giants Play Well in the Drizzle, Grosseteste Review, Harper's, The London Review of Books, The New Yorker, Ninth Decade, Numbers, oink!, Origin, Scripsi, Sulfur, Threepenny Review, ZYZZYVA.

All the poems here, some in variant drafts, have appeared in earlier collections:

The Sausage Master of Minsk (Villeneuve, Montreal, 1977); *A Calendar of Airs* (The Coach House Press, Toronto, 1978); *Storm over Hackensack* (Moyer Bell Ltd., Mt. Kisco, N.Y., 1985); *On Johnny's Time* (Pig Press, Durham, England, 1988); *Dainties & Viands* (Galloping Dog Press, Newcastle, 1989); *Earthquake Weather* (Moyer Bell Ltd., 1989)

The author wishes to thank the editors of some of these journals and the publishers of these several books for taking my work up and encouraging me early on. Most especially: Fred Louder and Robyn Sarah, Michael Ondaatje, Eliot Weinberger, Wendy Lesser, Clayton Eshleman, Peter Craven and Michael Heyward, Richard Caddel, Peter Hotchkiss, Britt Bell and Jennifer Moyer.

For going through my early work and helping me select poems for this volume I am indebted to: Michael O'Brien, William Corbett, Christian Wiman, Mark Payne, and Andrew Osborn.

Caroline Lander saw most of these poems first, and in the rough, and for her always forthright mixture of enthusiasm, scorn or indifference, my love and gratitude.

Contents

WEST

When the Master was in Ch'i, he heard the Shao music and for
three months he forgot the taste of meat . . .

– THE CONFUCIAN ANALECTS

If you're not nervous, you're not paying attention.

– MILES DAVIS

EAST

Where Souls Go

No telling where: down the hill
and out of sight—
soapbox derby heroes in a new dimension.
Don't bother to resurrect them
unless some old newsreel clip
catches them shocked
with a butter knife in the toaster.
Countless snaps and episodes in space
once you hit the viewfinder that fits.
It's a lie anyway, all Hollywood—
the Mind is a too much thing
cleansing itself like a great salt sea.
Rather, imagine them in the eaves

among pigeons
or clustered round the D train's fan
as we cross the bridge to Brooklyn.
And make that a Friday night
July say. We are walking past
the liquor store to visit our love.
Two black boys are eating Corn Doodles
in the most flamboyant manner possible.
She waits, trying
to have the best song on as we arrive.
The moon is blurred.
Our helicopters are shooting at fieldworkers.
The Mets are down 3–1 in the 6th.

Show Business

That was a book I think you
were the Duchess
me the Stableboy
I remember now the horseapples
and itchy wool it was never that way
but God were you ever a Sireen
that I do remember and how the Townsfolk

flushed you'd have thought a gram
of niacin was in them instead of you
on your way out of the Butcher's
with half a roast and some mustard
under your arm turning suddenly
with that look of sexual malice I think
you were rich but I forget who

it was betrayed whom and were we
in love the Players most of them are
still in the Directory we could phone
and ask that is except your Sister
who perished poor thing the Actress
who took her part was gallant but missed
that delicacy of nature which killed

your Sister whom I do remember
but the rest what was between us
how the garden smelled the electric
storms were we or not I wonder
how we are punished for forgetting
or let go numb
somewhat more smooth charming and mean

Blue at 4 p.m.

The burnish of late afternoons
as winter ends—
this sadness coming on in waves is not round
and sweet
as the doleful cello

but jagged, intent
finding out places to get through the way wind
tries seams
and cracks of the old house, making
the furnace kick on

or the way his trumpet
sharks
through cloud and paradise shoal, nosing
out the dark fillet
to tear apart and drink his own

From FDR Drive the Children of Whitman Gaze Up

Lavender smoke from the Con Ed stacks
assembles its tufts
into bubbles of thought (viz., the funnies) high
                    over the chilly river
and her bridges,
monuments of clunkish whimsy from an Age of Boom.

For the sky is synchronous this evening;
through the windshield its vistas
exactly right.
                    Yes and speed too is sweet
at the golden hour,
dipping under viaducts and out
into heraldic light on the bounce

off Citicorp's roof,
the only pentahedron in sight,
up way up
            high for a street-rooted thing
but no kin of sky

as are those puffs wind
fails to scatter
but simply hang there like smudged zeppelins
one might be induced to
think scented
                    while small craft higher yet
crisscross
aimlessly over the factories and luncheonettes
of Queens
            clearly beyond this spectacle
and thou,
dreamily seeking your exit.

Song

No one said
jiggle stuck syllables till the sow
drops piglets

and we'll buy
you a cottage way back in the trees
with fat fat June bugs

that slap the screens
No one said
grub your noggin night

and day
and here's a stack of 78's
by the one the only

Memphis Minnie
Sing for your supper and look
what you get

potato eyes and a helium crepe
And for dessert, Monsieur?
Sincere best wishes

Put in another slug
and I'll tell you what else
No one said

Boo

The Last Big Snow

(MONTREAL, 1977)

I

     She snowed
a night, a day
and another night, laying down deafness
as she went
and deafness again on top of
what she had let down
as she wound continually out of herself.

     And when she was done
she pulled
a wind onto the town, routing
snow into spindrift
off the mortar between bricks,
then blowing it back down.
     Cats
threw cats
   off each shed's sweetest angle.

II

The week that freighters slept in the ice
a day from port,
and the dove at our window
coo'd till first light,
my love gave herself over to making a broth.
With the fluid and pith of pale legumes
she came on a savor
     that visited our rooms
like a certain thought.

[8]

Those nights near the turning
when beacons on snowplows flashed until dawn,
and caravans of trucks
brought snow to the river as snow fell
on the river,
my love gave herself over to the making of broth
while I, in turn,
stirred until thick my greasy soup.

Winter Branches

FOR RALPH MILLS, JR.

A net of capillaries, veins, the full moon
beats through
    the sky late winter
between sunset and night

more clarifying to the spirit
than the ancient Chinese glazes, tea dust,
    plum shade,
the celadons from Hangchow

that take hold of the mind,
fastening it;
    and when a bird shoots through
between shadow and snow, branch and roof,

the heart tracks it
washed in a pleasure so distilled,
    so exquisite and sharp,
as to seem a kind of ecstasy

Evening, Out of Town

Falling, falling
until breath wanders out of itself, transforms and is lost
and then there is simply a disembodied pulsing
a small dark bird
a nub

Boats
with a single lamp ride the water's lip, and the quiet
keeps vigil for a small intrusion: the shadows
presage so many things
but no intrusion, only some memory unhoused

Ahasuerus

There was no hazard so we left off
when night fell.
The wind spoke too slowly to fathom.
Voices, lights
drifted away from us like a cloud of gnats.

I can remember that first morning
when we woke athwart the world.
Even the light had its own strange scent.
Any sudden shadow of bird or branch
triggered a shock between our genitals and spine.

The worst, naturally, was the waiting.
Whiskey, chess and sentences
that broke off
only to reconnect past memory's gate.
The gardener scything out there was wild himself.

When the girls arrived we swam to the point, fucked
and walked back
along the gravel road to the highway.
The sun drew out the echoing in our blood
but by then we were already listening like tourists.

After a winter the villagers,
dull salacious eyes in tiny heads, warmed
to us, confided to us
their peculiar gossip and lore.
Their wives brought cookies.

We learned nothing.
The cookies tasted like rancid dust.

But when we looked in the mirror
we were both ourselves and otherwise.
Spirit and flesh played blithely in each other's yard.

Canada Geese in New Jersey

       Headed north
on the sodded-over trolley track
to Coytsville
       or until carbons blew free
of the brain stem, out
both ears, settling like soot on wet grass

I heard a honk and made to duck
but two geese slanted past—
getting the hell out of here,
honking all night up the Hudson Valley.

Just like that: *honkhonk*:
a honk about as straight as their necks.
Two big geese can scare up the dead.
Then they're gone.

       Azalea blossoms stir,
like so many tiny nightgowns.

The creases in the schoolboy's pegged wool slacks
blow flat against his ankles
as he puffs uphill in the Bronx. The day is
raw and new. He didn't do his Latin.

Below and to the east smoke braids
and drifts farther east. Levering and stoking
out there grown men in coveralls slog through
the dead hours, while in their lunch pails

bologna sweats. A bird is in the schoolboy's head:
Shelley's skylark. Ha, that prink
never lurched uptown on the El with squads
of plump domestics lost in romance comics

and down each night
past the Italian cookie factory, its sigh-
fetching smells. Life
is a tunnel the kid's soul spills out of—

blithe crystal missile
kissing down in a meadow, high
over the Bay of Naples.
Girls are there

in bright cotton dresses pulled just past
the knee. In gestures ritual,
tacit and wild,
they offer him glances, then sweet things to eat.

This is the place our friend shall run
the circuit of every glad thing, flare
and perish
    exquisitely.

Where Galluccio Lived

Get all of it, boys,
every brick,
so the next big storm blows out
any ghost left with the dust.

In that closet of air the river
wind gnaws at
was where the crucifix hung;
and over there

by the radio and nails,
that's where Galluccio kept
with his busted leg
in an old, soft chair

watching TV and the cars
go past.

 Whole floors,
broken up and carted off . . .

Memory stinks,
like good marinara sauce.
You never get that garlic smell
out of the walls.

On the Way Home to Jersey One Night

The same old stories whip around
and around,
streaking the air between dark buildings,
breaking apart in the updraft.

A million tough chances
and Dina's bad back—
a nebula of complaint and spattered talk
flying apart in the wind:

the wind off the Hudson,
wrapping itself round the Hotel New Yorker,
riding the aluminum twigs
of a cyclone fence—

something about the wind,
how it roots around in the passageways and lots,
a kind of animal;
and in the night itself,

so dark,
as if everything had been washed out of it—
absence, an unearthly absence,
like space.

And who is it out there
in the shadows and doorways,
at every window and busted skylight?
Who is it I sense there out on his rounds,

keeping the ledger,
taking the last soiled scraps of it in?

Art & Youth

Pliny said these lights in the grass are stars;
a man walking home from his day's labor
needn't lift his head skyward to tell the signs.
Before the heavens were busy with Sputniks
and idiot beeps that say *hey!* to far-off worlds
we ran at the lights with jars. We ran and ran
until nothing was left of our bodies to spend.

An ache so sweet was born those nights
in the heat, in the grass, at summer's waning
that we try for it years later in the dance
of lust and lust's passing.
   Poor Swinburne,
dithery and gallant in great drafty rooms,
would have had this ache flogged back into him,
but the heart is soon corrupted
and love's accoutrements grow fierce.

Vikings of the Air

Our skycraft rides too low to clear the heights—
    Dump the goods, you scallywags, save this balloon.
The pink rocks of Arcadie fall out of sight:
down down through moving stacks of cloud
our plunder falls like defused bombs.
Peasant skulls explode in fields of chard.
The cargo we bartered bravely for is lost.
Screwed again. Heft brought us low
and close to jeopardy. Below, each spring
herring fishermen are likewise sunk by greed.
Happily, air is what fuels our craft
and we can buy air by dropping what we must.
    Give them back what we fought like gods for.
Make height, you bastards. The wind
drives east toward the sea, and our wives
are sure to brighten as our craft comes into sight.

Afternoon in the Middle Kingdom

Dust storms from the Gobi sack Peking.
The northwest suburbs vanish in a cloud.
Soon cheery bicyclists in thongs
sneeze up and down Great Boulevard,
falling headlong into ginkgos.
Cold sand wanders into hallways;
for weeks grit is found in spoon drawers,
in woolens, rose-petal jam and cats.
The French ambassador has a snit
about the joyless life. His wife,
whose perfume brings giggles at market,
once again tells her husband of Moon
Porcelain. But the city is gray
and vast, the parks in disrepair
and the sea three hours by rail.

Three Love Poems

I *Valentine Out of Season*

Way back, little kumquat, bold petunia
mine. I say

way way back past the bleached cartoons
doilies and particles of moth

a world and a world again removed
from the ventilator hum

of the brain
avenging itself on the spinal cord

where the heat of the moon
is a pale red cloud on the amnesiac's brow—

From that far place I shiver and arrive
in you, my singular love

while even yet the lunging parts
of us splash and collide down the amazing flume

II *Pinned*

The ways water finds to undo
    the bonds of solid things:

you move across my flank,
    the ground turns strange;
your sylph-gang churns a breeze
    and my beanie's propeller
ticks the air morosely;
    two steps and I'm out of breath;
morsels of scrod and aspic
    drop unchewed to my plate.

Wrestlers work this way:
    they uproot you from earth
and take you back down,
    tied insolubly to their wills.

III *Invitation*

　　　　Ah, but Anthea, these shallows
are for children and they are long asleep.
The lake, so black and still, beseeches us
with coolness to cut our bodies through.
The opposite bank is not too far
and what small creatures prowl below can but wonder
at that turbulence our legs and arms churn up.

　　　　Mosquitos will soon bleed us
pale as the moon, nowhere to be found, while lights
and music from the cabin above offer nothing,
less than nothing, retreat to our scabbards of fiction.

Come—
　　　　our friends, friends by rote,
can puzzle to themselves
while we undress and swim far out
to the cool black eye of our histories.

Boxing on Europe's Most Beautiful Beach

A slow breeze north from Africa
would not allow the surf to chill
our modest *vinho,* up
to its neck in sand, on time
to wash down heavy farm rolls
and oleaginating cheese-of-the-hills.

She surprised me, as bantam weights
can do, with a neat left cross
to the side of the head
and thought to make a combination
with a straight right hand.

I ducked. At my back an igneous
bluff loomed burnt-sienna.
What was I to do? I counter-
punched, just above the elastic
waist of her skyblue underpants.
Down she went, doubled
like an embryo in sand.

Her arm, raised to shield
her eyes from the winter sun
or me, was dark, the flesh mingling
nicely with the abundant strands
of down from her wrist to elbow.

    Her breasts,
like troubled engines, rose
and fell as she worked to find
her breath. Her face, as soft
in line as any Burne-Jones painted
except for the gag-tooth
and chin, a trifle Slovak,

changed from a pellucid blue
to red to the kind of pink
uncommon but for the magnolia.

Reluctant to turn away,
though courtesy required it,
I brought the wine and rolls.
Is reciprocity not the kernel
of all Confucius taught? So when
she knocked the tendered cup
out of my hand, hope for perfect
accord spilt there too. And yet,
with unmistakable sweetness,
she did say,
                    Hit me again.

The Device

You see, it's a total environment fits like a shoe.
What don't belong slips through
our *solar wind* feature just blows 'er out.
Not like those weeds crack cement and rune the conduit—
none of that.

So how do we know what don't belong?
(You're a regular philosopher, buddyboy.)
Because *you* programmed it, that's how.
And here's the beauty part:
you can forget or change your mind like a coked-up
        dolly on roller skates

but this little baby won't.

The Interior Decorator on Sunday

Those strange and translucent scampi in lantern hats
who graze then vanish into night's big hole
are here, shorted-out, hard
to pick up in the neutral air,
but afloat between ceiling and carpet.
No, they are not. They are off
across the ravine of bison grass and dead shoots,
over the boulevard and gone
to spin or park on their filament's last inch.

On the wall is a spot: the painter sneezed
. . . or dirt,
or it is a cousin back from the dead
yearning to touch brows.
The spot is not monochrome; red is with that gray.
It is . . . a cell beset by virus.
Really, I don't know. So much business thins me out.
And now voices approach: they are spheres,
textured.

The Sausage Master of Minsk

I was sausage master of Minsk;
young girls brought parsley to my shop
and watched as I ground
coriander, garlic and calves' hearts.

At harvest time they'd come with sheaves:
hags in babushkas, girls plump
as quail, wrapped in bright tunics,
switching the flanks of oxen.
Each to the other, beast and woman,
goggle-eyed at the market's flow.

My art is that of my father:
even among stinking shepherds, bean-
brained as the flocks they tend, our
sausages are known. The old man
sits in back, ruined in his bones, a scold.

So it was my trade brought wealth.
My knuckles shone with lard, flecks
of summer savory clung to my palms.
My shop was pungent with spiced meat
and sweat: heat from my boiling pots,
my fretful labors with casings,
expertly stuffed. Fat women in shawls
muttered and swabbed their brows.
Kopeks made a racket on my tray.

But I would have none of marriage:
the eldest son, no boon,
even with the shop's renown, was
I to my parents. Among mothers
with daughters, full-bottomed, shy,
I was a figure of scorn.

In that season when trade was a blur,
always, from the countryside, there was one,
half-formed, whose eyes, unlike
the haggling matrons' squints, roamed
and sometimes found my own.
And of her I would inquire.
Before seed-time they always returned.

Tavern men speak freely of knives,
of this, of that. Call me a fool.
For in spring I would vanish
to the hills and in a week return,
drawn, remote, my hair mussed,
interlaced with fine, pubescent yarn.

Lighting Bugs

A cruel word at eventide
and night zips up
like a spider's retreat.

Go back to your febrile
needlework.
        We shall not
be chasing lightning bugs
in the tall grass tonight.

Put the whiskey on the shelf
and let us speak calmly
of money.

Storm over Hackensack

This angry bruise about to burst
on City Hall
will spend itself fast
so fluid and heat may build again.

But for a moment the light
downtown
          belongs someplace else,
not here
or any town close.

Look at the shoppers, how palpable
and bright
against gathering dark
like storied figures in stereoscope.

This is the gods' perpetual light:
    clarity
    jeopardy
        change.

Meat

How much meat moves
Into the city each night
The decks of its bridges tremble
In the liquefaction of sodium light
And the moon a chemical orange

Semitrailers strain their axles
Shivering as they take the long curve
Over warehouses and lofts
The wilderness of streets below
The mesh of it
With Joe on the front stoop smoking
And Louise on the phone with her mother

Out of the haze of industrial meadows
They arrive, numberless
Hauling tons of dead lamb
Bone and flesh and offal
Miles to the ports and channels
Of the city's shimmering membrane
A giant breathing cell
Exhaling its waste
From the stacks by the river
And feeding through the night

Sunday at Fletcher's Field

Ruder light was taken by sail
to the bishop of Seville
than this benison
suddenly on us like oil
pressed warm from olives.

The west goal mouth
is free for an instant but the kick
is high. Two wings
in green shorts cry out.

But the ball stays up. The sun
on its way down
has swallowed the world.
The park's suffused,

the shirts and the dogs,
with the burnish of Corelli's horns.

Ghosts

Ghosts
    loop-the-loop like mad.
    Impassive
to our little shames
they somersault all day.

Aether's their stuff; go
they must.
    Will,
even to the gunners
among them,
    is less than air,
    less
even
    than the shape
their noses
carved
prow-like
    in their day. Relentless
as beavers
who chew or die
they gambol
in our oats,
    buzz
our marshdreams

move & move
    through
    and under us
who loved
   them
    helplessly
      in life.

Poetics

I have loved the air outside Shop-Rite Liquor
on summer evenings
better than the Marin hills at dusk
lavender and gold
stretching miles to the sea.

At the junction, up from the synagogue
a weeknight, necessarily
and with my father—
a sale on German beer.

Air full of living dust:
bus exhaust, airborne grains of pizza crust
wounded crystals
appearing, disappearing
among streetlights and unsuccessful neon.

Like Cities, Like Storms

Like cities, like storms

these alto and tenor men
blow back cool legato or a rope of cries
against a world pouring down
so hard and fast

the bass and drums are about to fly
off the beat
and lose the soloist orbiting
round it

but don't, somehow
thirty, forty years ago at the Royal
Roost, Five Spot or studio
in Hackensack.

With the owner counting heads
and the kid
down from Yale working his way up
his girlfriend's thigh

the rhythm men keep holding on

a foot off the ground,
but holding.

Staying Home from Work

That is a mower from the city
you hear in the park
so mild a day no heat
nowhere to be till lunch
nothing to think
money
nobody
lie still and listen
like the boy did
long ago
listening to neighbors mow
sniffing summer through the curtains

Such care the city takes
not to let grass grow
too long
and should you fall again
to dreaming
no one will reproach you
or come seek you out
to put you off this sweetness
so rare
so minor a key were it music
if fabric
would come apart in your hands

WEST

On Johnny's Time

When Johnny goes out
he's careful what gets into his Time.
He likes Time plain,
the better to taste it run out of him
like water out holes
in the Old Town's corroded pipe.

— *What sort of business you in?*
the good burgher always asks John.
— *Monkeybusiness,* is what John likes to tell him,
and won't crack a smile, ever.
That's John.
But when Johnny goes out

on Johnny's own Time
he's out there doing the only one thing:
he's burning off all the stillborn Johnnys
that hatched in his head in the night.
And that John, he won't ever come home,
not until he's right.

Art & Life

That's really quite a lovely figure
you bring off
with those several morphemes
arrayed so that when taken up by the mind
they deploy into a kind of umbrella
ranged round an emotion
fleeting and delicate as to seem
the afterimage of an emotion
or of a dream perhaps
or nothing at all,
but always with that high finish,
your signature —
the delightful origami of an exiled prince.

But not nearly so good as
the face
of the Italian beauty, a TV star
on a warm morning
in an alley below Mission, smelling
something much too intimate
underneath the smells of a poor, close street
with its clotheslines, warm brick
and radios pouring
out dj Spanglish, trumpets and love songs

while the dark, blocky girl,
cheekbones and features of an ancient
stone mask, walks past
with her baby, sneaking a look
at those darling lace half-socks, little
tits pushed up high, and hair teased
same as the photos in beauty
parlor windows.

     —Another side
of the city,
   —I tell the Signora,
uno altro aspetto.
    Her eyes
gone a bit wild, and the mouth

not so nice.

Earthquake Weather

She's talking to herself
or somebody
spasm talk
heaving
broken apart
as it escapes her weather

She can slip in there
when the air's right
and lay her stripe down
red
along your nerve-snake's sheathing

Mrs. B.
she forgot her medication
now she's *on*
flinching
at the rejoinder
or blow

matted hair
and chewed red nose
that's her
hard done by
. . . husband
mother . . .
cruel fat daughter
money
always money

pleading her case down Clayton
solo
in the fog

past the old chow
puzzling her scent through
Mrs. B.

faces staring
as the bus makes its turn
she'll lay her stripe down
when the air gets still
she'll slip right in
and make you breathe
wrong

Sunday in November

And who were they all in your sleep last night
    chattering so
you'd think that when you woke
the living room would be full of friends and ghosts?

But you see, nobody's here, no one but you
    and the room's nearly bare
except for Paddy's playstring all covered in dust
and a bottle of tinted air.

Pop and Lola, the sullen little clerk from the store,
    and eight or ten more. Now
which were the dream ones and who did you meet that was
    real?
You were, for the most part, you.

Such a big room: how nice to be alone in it
    with the one lit bulb and dying plant,
the day so large and gray outside,
dogs running through it in circles, buses, shouts.

And later on where will you take her?
    Up to the rock. And what will you see there?
    Roofs and the bay. Have you a song to sing her?
    The wind will do and she'll think it's me.

But who were they all in your sleep last night
    first one then the next
with their menace, wild semaphore and lusts?
I hardly know where you find the strength

come morning.

The Lunatic of Lindley Meadow

At nightfall, when the inquisitive elves in elf-pants
wander over the ridge with chummy screed,
the snaps of the beak your hand becomes cease,

and evening's last fungo dwindles
high over the spruce, for an instant getting lost
in one band of sky turning dark under another,

falling back into view, falling
out of the sky, *pop*, a dead wren in his mitt. *Let's
get home*, the big boy says, *Mom'll holler*.

The car horns along Fulton subside with the dark,
the big felt-lined dark: bright little logos and cars
set in black felt while still pulsing light,

a lid on top. And see, here he comes now,
Conga Lad, pleasing the elves, who come close but not too,
making the birds go way. Time to start home,

so clean it up nice and blow germs off your pouch—
the nice warm room, the smell in the wool.

What It Takes

He stared for hours
at the cat
taking his ease under the calla leaf
or fog
pour in late afternoon
whelming the tower on the hill

how bird   truck   or shout
wind & light
scored day the way the music
roll in a nickelodeon's scored
and what it played in the mind

or the young Bill Evans
before Scott LaFaro died
playing
        "My Foolish Heart"
again and again
fennel, lobelia   shadow & flies

however many times it takes

Friday Monday in the Haight

The gray man at the door
of his rental TV shop pauses,
bent
with pain shooting through like the express

at a local stop. Gas
maybe
or cancer working the membranes.
A cloud of spider motes

swaddles his head,
evaporates.
The gallery of Zeniths in half-light
. . .

There's a real deal in back
for burn-outs, students and pensioners:
a black & white set,
1958.

Deep in its cool metal sheathing
a ghost constellation
traces itself among atoms—
half-blown neon in a snowstorm.

It is Perry Como,
velvet-throated Italian barber,
and he is singing
    Quando Quando Quando

through eternity.

Warm Night in February

It smells of summer out,
she said
        in Safeway's parking lot,
tilting her head
to reach more air.

There is a kind of wave
that falls upon us
unawares.
        I cannot tell you
how it comes or when
but we are left there broken,
our voices everywhere scattered.

Tenderloin: An Etymology

Electric here is closer to the skin.
Receptor hairs on top
tell anything,
givegivegiving the nerve.
                    Thus, tender.

Loin is warm;
even at night it's warm. Sleep
with fists in there tight
if you're cold.
                    No hotel is too cold.

Loin is the hub,
its breathing ceaseless. Within
protein gathers unto its template,
pieces falling
                    that enzymes may burn.

And then the smell

September, with Travelers

Only a moon ago, coolness at evening—
a delicate astringent.
Now sunflower stalks routed to earth
and the passes treacherous.

It seems only last week
those sunsets,
like gardens of sky in all their extravagance,
kept on without end,

night-tinted smoke flooding the valleys,
the lightest of breezes,
trembling sage.

Now the curtains drawn
earlier each evening and the dinner wine
left half-finished,
while outside the pine boughs and cedar
take on new life in wind,

their bounding shadows
an elaborate display on the walls.

One guest after another passing through.
A few quiet hours here,
a long, difficult journey from town,
before heading on.

What is the expression?
Gathering one's thoughts—
as if kindling or hen-of-the-woods,
or perhaps something rarer still.

Rueful smiles,
their dear, aging faces . . .
Never time enough

before having to head back,
back to where they left off.

Old Movies

Fueled with violins, the luscious soundtrack
pulls the old movie down the line
with its cargo of lovers   limo   and guns
till our hearts break
and the exit doors open on goodness and hope.

Goodbye, my love, goodbye.
Light pricks us
and we bleed from a thousand tiny holes
opalescent air draining out of us
night rushing in.

Disappointment

A faint smell of urine
embroidering that bouquet of mold the big cushions
give off days the fog won't lift,

and a shelf of bone
growing out over the eyelids like evening's shadow
across a field of corn—

The whole parade
leaking out from your shoulders, bequeathing
to the groin a pang of distance;

then that metallic taste in the mouth
and a voice you had let yourself believe
was dead

close now by your ear, intimate and sweet:

> *Well, well, well,*
look *what we have here.*

Lock Shop

Frank punched steel stamps into key bows
then duped them on the grinder
for thirty-odd years,
just to keep off from dead-bolt or cylinder work.
He never did learn how to locksmith—

thirty-odd years and the old nail pounder
still couldn't figure it out:
just the hammer, drill and a big smile
for whatever lady it was up front.
Besides, he liked how hard metal bit into soft.

The last day Frank wore powder-blue dacron slacks
and a necktie with little birds knit in.
He had coffee like always with the machinists at break,
kissed both secretaries, kissed DeLois
        at the Trouble Desk,
and left.

        Now John says he's had it;
took a job in the desert, down around Blythe:
a new correction facility
not a hundred miles from that land he bought
right along the Colorado.
He'll still be State so won't hurt on his pension.

John used to locksmith over at Vacaville,
the biggest prison on earth.
Told me how one time there he ran into Charlie Manson.
—*Was he crazy?* I asked.

—*Crazy?* John says and gives me this look.

Crazy?

—*Hell yes, he was crazy.*

Sunday in September

Oh I dunno Ma walk around town I guess
check out the arugula at Tony Pro's

then head along to the sea and back
or what the sky has going

late one Sunday afternoon toward fall
high over the Panhandle and college spires

gray as ever but just now another gray
ask Turner—Turner *Who & How Much?*

air cooler and the breeze very fresh
you peek into the half-light

of a corner bar, color TV flickering
heads bent over drink or tilted up

in ritual tropisms of talk or the game—
a diorama the new museum paid too much for

Ebenezer Californicus

Don't make me go out eat goose
be nice get a headache
all right?
because the sun's so strong
so warm delish the back of my neck
making mutinous the wee city-states
that dot it—
goosebumps of intrigue, of the possible

Terrible people
up&down the street terrible people
smiling
     the smiles of greed
     the mooncalf's grin
     the Bob Hope Holiday Leer of Delight
the smile of the broken,
hurt
     pullulating:
     not six weeks out of the can
     like drunk at 8 a.m.

     that smile

—Maddy crifsmuss, brudder
Stare shhange?
        O Christ
O
    Merry WhackWhack, Mrs. QuackQuack

      Write soon

       Love

       Baby Teapot

An Autumnal Sketch

What to make of them, the professors
in their little cars,
the sensitive men paunchy with drink
parked at the fence
where the field begins and the suburb ends?

If there is a mallard in the reeds
they will take it.
They will take it and make it their own,
something both more than a duck
and less.

They so badly want a poem,
these cagey and disheartened men
at the edge of the field.
And before they turn back for supper
they shall have one.

Ye Olden Barge

As Plot rounded the corner
ants got him,
twirling in his sugar and pith

took the ground out
from under him,
tunneling, putting down eggs

dismantled the Protein Church
within sight of Denouement—
our faith, all of our hopes . . .

To get from here to there
in the grand curve,
every inch a storm of bites.

Hack

Pigman dispatches us across the city
as barmen shout *last call.*
In a tiny room above Foo Hong's he sweats.

Only the men with eyes of glue are left.
A kid gusts past, smoking
staccato in his fantailed old heap.

The Pig tells a joke, something
about one of the dwarfs and Snow White,
a vile, Pig sort of joke;

but the vileness recedes, leaving behind
an image of the two of them:
naked, breathless, limbs entwined,

free now of the story's landscape,

dissolving into night.

The Inland Passage

(JUNEAU, 1973)

Your sadnesses reign unbroken
as the north coast sky,
from the Charlottes up
the inland passage
where the weather stays hard;
a place the Tlingits fish,
a tribe almost bereft of art.
Bars open their doors at six
and fill up with white men,
bellies full of scrambled eggs,
chasing the grease with rye.

And when the weather breaks
in country like that, where
spring and autumn don't seem
to change a thing, a curious
distress comes to most faces
and the mountains, disrobed
of their mists, loom
above the town
with an unreal acuity.
It was on a day like that
I left.

The Fourth of July

(MᶜCALL, IDAHO, 1985)

Mountain blue on the powerline,
preening,
as the big C-119 heads out low over aspen
and yellow pine, dragging
slurry to Challis, up by Yankee Fork.

Idaho is burning.
Hot dogs on sale at the Merc.
Pleasure craft
tearing apart the morning lake
send osprey wheeling toward deeper woods.

Aspen, osprey —
haze over half the state:
on TV
the Atlanta infield green as old Technicolor
while cool still in the front room.

Under how many roofs, domes
of sky . . .

> Two boys on the ferry north,
> out of Seattle, spring '73,
> all pumped up
> and ready for somewhere
> with no way back from —
> the books   the fear   the girls
> reduced to a map of where they had to go.
>
> The Wickersham rocks
> as she threads the narrows,
> a day then a night to Ketchikan,

the rain turning heavy
near sundown.

You say how it's like acid,
you don't even know
what it is supposed to happen next anymore.
I don't even try to say.

Seems like nearly half the town
is sitting out there on the lake,
sipping beer,
waiting for dark.
Collins, one of the smoke jumpers off shift,
passes a joint
between boats to your old lady's ex,
fireworks suddenly exploding into bloom overhead,
colored flares dying before they hit the lake.

Past novelty and charm,
the best moves left for strangers,
moves to buy time,
we sneak looks at one another,
as if taking measure,
friend at friend,
each more and more coming to resemble his father.

Poppies in the Wind

The honeybee
painting himself his delight inside her
the both of them
adrift
tossing in fits of wind
petals of her knees
raised up around him
petal arms
encircling in shadow his cameo'd frenzy
hosts of them
open or clenched
waving
sheathed or half out
of their witch-hats
at May's meridian
drying like chicks in the air

Indian Summer Night: The Haight

        The 43 bus at Carl & Cole
steps on the comic's line
but applause and laughter
waft up the lane.
        A *ranger* on the grass
bestirs himself,
spooked

    then barks back a laugh of his own,
an unwholesome laugh,
stiffening the neighbor cats.

The summer my sister worked at Palisades Park
I'd stay awake till midnight,
listening.
When the breeze in the maples was right
you could hear her

my sister,
over the loudspeaker a quarter mile away
telling barkers, patrons and freaks,
everybody,
the last voice before the lights went out,

— *Thank you. Good night.*

Before Winter

Another six peaches down in the night
and yellowjackets
swarming a rat my darling
boy got hold of
that *pockateeka*, chewing himself
in the shade
oh, don't you
sting my good boy's tongue
and leave him choke, no
he is my joy
as day breaks
warm waves of it
first one then the next then the . . .
each freighted,
denser than the last,
with pieces of night,
of day:
            the aroma of asphalt steaming
after a rain
and the corner vedette
fussing with a pear from the bin, or how
you touched me right then . . .
and faces
voices issuing from those faces
running up&down
the vibraphone of me in sheets
and there's my
own voice, somehow
got separated in the crowd
I say
            Let me see down from a
very high place,
not tethered here by need

I tell my boy
                    Be careful,
manjelaketta,
take especial care
the yard is too too wild

Bay Lullaby

Tuesdays are bad for sausage and flowers
rain
sweeping in off the sea, foghorns
lowing like outsize beasts
shackled to cliffs at the mouth of the Bay

You hear them from under the movie marquee
before going in to dry
off in plush, alone
behind two old ladies, that song of a wanton from long ago
"Temptation," filling the empty room

Across the city's northwest quadrant
two, maybe three miles in
drifting through holes in the traffic and rain
you hear them warning ships off the rocks
moaning like fettered gods

Lilies begun to curl
and meat gone sad at the delicatessen
trays of wurst
fat seeping into the skins
before Thursday delivery and the big weekend

As morning's first trolley clears the track
the cat's petite snores
sweat beaded on my love's upper lip
you still hear them out there in the dark
mingling their calls in the rain

Dispatch

Be still

Say nothing

Ask nothing of anyone

The ego is a ghost ship

Don't hurt your bones trying

This is only the end of a long day in June

The picnickers head home, feverish and drunk

Trolley

The trolley runs out to the sea
swivels
        and comes back
under the sidewalk where Crazy Jack
lays hands on faithless aerial rats.
His head's on springs.

The sea is colored mercury.
The trolley swivels
        and comes back
past skinny sidewalk trees
where almost no one is
but the corner grocerman, his cupcakes
and linoleum.

The trolley runs out to the sea
swivels
        and comes back
'cross avenues that once were dunes
and crones now perch,
pelicans in chubby shoes.
They're waiting for the trolley

runs out to the sea
swivels
        and comes back
to crewcut Rituh,
she's a butch little teasuh
sheezuh

swivels
        and comes back
to MickeyMike
raking the grill with his spatula

He's got the Cuban beans
          authentic sauce
          whadayaneed
MickeyMike

          and comes back
to slick black kids with skinny hips
cow-eyed couples from far away
Chinese roots for a windy day
the mile-long circus where no one pays

and runs out to the sea.

The Tree

Pinch a branch to see if it's quick
or else the thing'll just stand
for who knows how long
sun, wind, frost, chafing it, dogs
pissing at the base
birds nesting up high where leaves had been

while the years blur
and the town next door's evacuated
so the kids don't turn stupid
from the water that solvents leached into
or testicle cancer
diagnosed in the Mayor on down

Cape Canaveral is renamed Eric Dolphy
your friends all swell, turn
ugly then drop
after their cute little girls grow up to fuck brutes
marry them and breed

but that shield of bark
photons roam the grain of
and pathogens try to corkscrew into
only to fall apart and dry . . .

because it would not bloom
because it would not die

the axman came

Sunset in Chinatown

The massive cable turns on its spool, pulling
carloads of tourists to the city's crest

       as the sun sits low
in the hills above Chinatown, exploding

suddenly in the window of Goey Loy Meats, high
along the top of the glass,

showering light over barbecued ducks—

a somehow elegiac splash
this evening, the last week before Labor Day

as if summer, in tandem with the sun,
were being pulled down

and away from us by the great spool's turning.

Thus, the sullen old man in his Mao cap
plucks the zither for change

on a crate outside the geegaw shop:

first, the ancient "Song of Cascading Water,"
followed by the plaintive
       "Lament of the Empress Ch'ou"

and even the bad little boy from Wichita Falls
trailing behind his parents in a sulk

registers that twinge

birds in the sky, insects and beasts no less
than the immortals

feel

when the plangent notes take shape in the air,
aligning their souls with Heaven and Earth.

Reflections by the Surging Wave Pavilion

Much of what's gathered in this collection now feels remote to me, sitting here poolside on a deck chair at a Phoenix airport hotel, waylaid for thirty-six hours after a missed connection. It is late afternoon, March, a few shadows beginning to creep in and the heat relenting a bit. The poolside is otherwise deserted, but somewhere, out of sight but close by, is a woman delivering a raw and unhappy mantra which involves sex, money, disappointment and betrayal. At first I thought I was eavesdropping on a phone conversation. Maybe I am, perhaps she's speaking into a dead cell phone. I understand many people do. The recurrence of certain themes and choice of epithet soon reveals the circular nature of her performance, which, in spite of the gamy bits, has begun to wear on me. Each new gust of displeasure begins with a corrosively nasal *an-GEL*, as if first stunning then reeling in her victim for another round of torment.

The younger poet in evidence throughout these pages would have been a good deal more intrigued with all this than I am. These poems, a number of them conceived, if not executed, over twenty-five years ago, were written in places like Vancouver-Island, Alaska, Idaho, Montreal, Portugal, New Jersey, Manhattan and, of course, San Francisco, where I've lived for the most part since 1981. What was I doing in these places? Working, traveling: all manner of work, none of it grand or especially interesting. It was a more forgiving time. One didn't need much. I never had much. In those days there was a lot of crashing around with friends, on mattresses, futons, the floor, in backyards. It was the great era for futon sales. I believe the notion was that if I led an interesting, modestly adventurous life I would write better poems. Certainly the vast tracts of empty, undirected time were critical. Perhaps that was the decisive thing: not to have allowed myself to be deflected. It had been quite clear to me, as early as fifteen or sixteen, that I was going to be a poet. I remember very clearly the excitement, of a neuromuscular sort, almost sexual, when I first began manipulating language, trying to pull emotions and color out of it.

The books I carried around in those days included Peter Whigham's translations of Catullus, the Anchor collection of shorter poems from the English Renaissance, the Penguin collection of Japanese verse and Ezra Pound's *Confucius to Cummings*. I first encountered Basil Bunting's poems in the last. One day, in 1970, when I was living for a time with my older brother in Greenwich Village, at his flat on Charlton Street, I came across the Fulcrum edition of Bunting's long poem *Briggflatts*. It was everything I wanted in poetry.

Then a most remarkable series of events unfolded. My brother told me to go home to see our parents in Jersey. That went badly. I got up at four or five the next morning, walked to the corner and hitchhiked to British Columbia, where I enrolled at the University of Victoria. I was going back to college because college seemed like something I knew how to do.

My brother's life was coming apart. He had gotten himself in trouble with gangsters and with the law. He was a wild, dear, buccaneering soul and it had all caught up with him. Inside of five months he would be dead, a suicide. I arrived in Victoria, slept in the park, found a place to kip, hitched to the west coast of Vancouver Island and took a job setting chokers and driving skidder in an illegal logging operation just below Estevan Point. It was like a movie: A party of native Canadians came out in canoes to challenge us and our boss paid them off in whiskey. The work itself was nasty and dangerous, the hours long, but it was a magnificent spot and you could see pilot whales sounding only a few hundred yards off shore.

When I returned to town I went up to the university and found, at the Department of English, the chap who was listed as teaching contemporary poetry. He was an unpleasant man, not stupid but clearly long ago compromised in some profound way. He explained to me that he would not be teaching the course, an elderly visiting English poet would be teaching it, someone I had probably never heard of: Basil Bunting.

It is dark in the hotel bar and quiet except for the TV. Judge Judy is reprimanding a young woman. The bartender says he doesn't like Judge Judy. He says she has it in for good-looking young women. He changes channels. It is the *Courage to Be Rich Show* with Suze Orman. He changes channels again: slow-motion videos of spectacular speedboat crashes.

Outside, airliners pass low across Phoenix's South Mountain and a row of office blocks, their glass and alloy cladding shimmering in the heat. I am on my way back from a writers' festival in the hills, en route to a semester-long job teaching poetry in a graduate writing program. From the deeply silly to the sillier still. It is only very recently that I've begun participating in these sorts of things. Even a couple of years ago it would never have occurred to anyone to invite me. I was not of that world, nor would I have chosen to be.

If there was a world I identified with, however marginally, or at least had some association with while writing these poems, it would probably have been the small-press world and its fugitive publications. That world too has its ridiculous hierarchies, operators and social networks, but it did provide a kind of sustenance away from university life, which I believed then, and still believe, poisonous to a writer.

I met the couple who published my first small collection while learning to set type one weekend out on a farm in Sooke, British Columbia. It's a pretty little thing, hand-set on a platen press nearly twenty-five years ago on a quiet, tree-lined street in the Greek quarter of Montreal. It seems, now, there was a lot of fine press work being done back then: chapbooks like this one, broadsides, pamphlets. One was more connected to the making of a book. With Momma eight months pregnant, I even had to do a fair share of pushing and pulling on that remarkably sturdy, efficient little press myself. In hand, finally, a made thing: word by word, syllable by syllable, letter by letter. The audience was only a handful, mostly other writers. There would be no reviews or prizes or job offers. No agents ringing up. No photo on the dust jacket looking earnest or seductive. There

was no dust jacket. I did it because I had to. It's all more compli-
cated than that, but there you have it. I had no idea of the conse-
quences of the decision I had made.

Across the highway from the hotel, amid the sun-baked deso-
lation of Phoenix, stands a large, elaborate shopping plaza in an
ersatz pagoda style. It is mostly vacant except for a couple of
restaurants, a market and the Chinese Cultural Center. There
are no pedestrians to speak of, but if there were, they would en-
ter directly through a gate guarded by two large Pi Xie, fantasti-
cal, griffin-like creatures. Inside, along a narrow swath, is a
garden of sorts with models of pavilions, springs, verandas and
reflecting pools from the Tang and Sung Dynasties, each a cele-
brated spot for contemplation "where scholars, poets and
painters would come for inspiration":

Rain Hat Pavilion Number Two   Spring on Earth
Maple Bridge Night Harbor   Poem Monument
Surging Wave Pavilion   Moon Gate Scenic Window
                                Star Gathering Pavilion

The sun is directly overhead. Six lanes of traffic pound by,
north and south, with the turnoff for 202 West to L.A. only a
couple of hundred yards up the road, right before you get to the
new Airport Marriott. To the east are two oddly shaped dark
mounds called the Papago Hills, beyond them the Superstition
Mountains, difficult to make out in the smog. There are sprays
of bougainvillea growing here and there, inexplicably, amid the
dust and asphalt and concrete. The Mexican gardener walks
past, giving me a suspicious look. It is very hot.

The older poet finds much to complain of here in the work of
the younger one. And I'd be a fool to believe the younger poet
wouldn't find plenty to complain of in my work, and in me. But
I'd like to think that he would almost certainly sit down gladly
here beside me on this bench by the side of the road, outside the
Moon Gate, in comradeship and wonderment.